EMBRACE
THE
BOOM

BILL JORDAN

Webster Falls Media™
Books · Films

www.WebsterFalls.com

Published by Webster Falls Media LLC
Wallace, N.C. · Burbank, CA

www.websterfalls.com
First Edition

ISBN (paperback): 978-0981687247
Library of Congress Control Number:
2021907718

Printed in the USA

This book is dedicated to my
Mom and Dad, and to the
millions of other members of our
Nation's "Greatest Generation"
...

I pray that we each earn these
lives for which they sacrificed.

Special Introduction

In *Embrace the Boom*, Bill Jordan takes us on a deeply personal journey, sharing his best practices for a more gratifying life as we grow older.

Knowing Bill for as long as I have, I can assure you he practices what he preaches.

Embrace the Boom is well worth the time investment to become more gracious, caring, accepting, courageous and, frankly, better.

- Mike Krzyzewski
Duke University and United States Senior National Team (2005 – 2016) Head Men's Basketball Coach

Get Ready to Launch

If you were born between 1946 and 1964, you are, by definition, a Baby Boomer. We were born to and raised by members of our Nation's Greatest Generation. Who, by the way, did nothing short of save the world.

We have knowledge, skills and stories.

There are over 76 million Baby Boomers in the USA alone.

I turned 65 in July, 2019, and I've noticed an attitude among some of my peers that portrays getting older as a bad thing. What's your option? As the saying goes: Never regret growing older. It is a privilege denied to many.

If you're reading this, I believe that you still have a mission. A reason for living.

Here's a crazy notion that I've got. I believe that at 65, I can get smarter, wiser, stronger.

BETTER. Yes. I believe that I can become a better human being.

I like to think that I am in the early part of the third act in the play that is my life. If you don't believe that you can better yourself, or you simply don't even want to try, then this book isn't for you.

But, if you are ready, then welcome to "Embrace the Boom".

This book looks at 15 practices in my life, that when I apply them daily, lead me to having a better life.

I have learned some things in my six-and-a-half years since leaving the radio business that I wish I had known and practiced when I was 16. I want to share these practices with you.

You may find many of them to be simple, but not easy. That's why they take "practice".

I believe that I am a better human when I adopt them. I hope you'll join me.

Live your life . . .

Forget your age . . .

Embrace the Boom.

"For as long as you live, keep learning how to live."

- Seneca

Embrace the Boom Practice # 1 - Attitude of Gratitude

"Gratitude turns what we have into enough." - Author Unknown

I begin my morning with an attitude of gratitude. And I keep it going as an undercurrent throughout my day.

I have always considered myself grateful, just as you have probably always considered yourself the same.

Of course, I'm thankful for my wife. I'm thankful for my daughter. For my grandchildren. For my health. And I know you are thankful for such blessings as well.

But, what I'm talking about is a mindful and focused attitude of gratitude. If you do it the first thing every morning, you'll be off to a stellar start.

Try to pick several things every morning for which to be grateful. Make them different every day. You won't run out of things. We always say that there is always something for which to be thankful. This is an opportunity to put that idea into play.

Here's what I'm getting at:

A few years ago, it dawned on me just how thankful I am for my senses. Seems obvious, but I had never really thought of them specifically. Everything that I enjoy in my life comes to me via my senses. Check in with your senses routinely.

What can you see?
What can you smell?
What can you hear?
What can you taste?
What can you feel?

As an example, when I step out on our back deck in the morning, my senses inventory may go something like this:

I can see a rabbit hopping across my yard.

I can smell the aroma of that first mug of strong coffee.

I can hear a mockingbird in a nearby tree, singing a song just for me.

I can taste that first bite of scrambled eggs.

I can feel the cool breeze on my skin.

Then, I employ the "Law of Opposites" and imagine those who cannot enjoy these simple pleasures that we all too often take for granted.

You understand the "Law of Opposites". You don't really appreciate your good health until you're sick. You don't appreciate being warm unless you've been cold. I took for granted being able to tie my shoes with ease until I broke a finger.

Be specific about those relationships and things for which you are grateful.

So, as you are probably grateful for your husband, be very focused as to WHY. Maybe it's the way he holds your hand, or that he makes you feel safe. Then, think of those who aren't blessed with a husband such as yours.

Soon you will take notice of more and more things throughout your day for which you are thankful.

I'll close out this Embrace the Boom Practice with one of my favorite quotes about gratitude:

"Gratitude is the healthiest of all human emotions. The more you express gratitude for what you have, the more likely you will have more for which to be grateful."

- Zig Ziglar

Embrace the Boom Practice # 2 - The Serenity Prayer

One of the key aspects of "Embracing the Boom" for me is the Serenity Prayer. You may be familiar with it since it's found in a million places. It goes like this...

"God, grant me the serenity to accept the things I cannot change, the courage to change the things I can, and for the wisdom to know the difference."

We're asking God for a calmness and tranquility to ACCEPT.

"Acceptance" is such a huge concept. There are so many things we cannot change. All the worry and regret in the world changes nothing at all.

It matters not what we said or didn't say. Did or didn't do.

Events and relationships don't always go the way we would like for them to.

Past, present and future. ALL contain stuff we cannot change.

Next.....the COURAGE to change the things we can.

Courage, typically, is an action. Yes, it starts with thought, but then it should lead to action.

What do you want to change?

Keep in mind, the only things you can truly change are those which apply to yourself.

And, finally, we ask in the Serenity Prayer the WISDOM to know the difference.

Wisdom is simply a matter of taking your own best advice. By the way, ever notice how we can get frustrated when we give unheeded advice to friends or family? But do we routinely accept our own advice? I believe that each of us knows the right thing to do, but do we do it?

No one else can live this prayer for you. Or define what serenity is to you. It's a personal decision that each of us has the freedom to make.

Which leads me to another Serenity Prayer. Maybe you've heard it.

"God, grant me the serenity to accept the people I cannot change, the courage to change the one I can, and the wisdom to know it's me."

We can't change the people around us. We can only change our reactions to them.

But we can't change THEM. Stop trying to. It'll save a lot of wear and tear on your psyche.

And there's a third Serenity Prayer that I didn't discover until a few months ago. And I love it...

"God, grant me the serenity to stop beating myself up for not doing things perfectly, the courage to forgive myself because

I'm working on doing better, and the wisdom to know that You already love me just the way I am."

There you go. Three Serenity Prayers.

I hope you will find strength and tranquility in them. I know I do.

Embrace the Boom Practice # 3 - The Golden Rule

Well, of course! We've known the Golden Rule ever since we were little kids!

"Do unto others as you would have them do unto you."

Be nice to people. Sure, that's a great and noble notion. But, there's something beyond that.

From people I don't know, I enjoy and appreciate their courtesy, being nice and polite to me. But, from trusted friends and family, I want more.

Oh, I want the kindness and the courtesy, but I also want and need their honesty. I want the honesty of people whom I hold in high regard.

When someone who really knows me, takes me aside and asks: "Are you really thinking this through? This path you're on, are you really sure about this? What you just said to them, do you really think that was the smart thing to say?"

When people whom I really look up to, admire and respect, come to me and guide me out of a loving and honest perspective, I really appreciate that. I value and cherish their wisdom.

Now, I may take their advice or not, but I want that from them.

We can be honest and kind at the same time. We don't have to beat each other over the head with our honesty.

By the way, based on personal experience, whenever someone brags about the fact that they can be "brutally honest".....watch out. Because what I've learned is that they tend to be more proud of their brutality rather than their honesty.

I trust that my cherished friends and family desire honesty from me as well.

I'm simply suggesting that you look at the Golden Rule a little bit differently than you may have before.

Bill Jordan

Just being honest.

Embrace the Boom Practice # 4 - Stay in the Present

I want to begin by sharing a number with you. 28,848.

I'll get back to that number. Promise. Kind of important.

This may be the toughest practice of them all for me. It's that simple notion we've heard so many times:

STAY. IN. THE. PRESENT.

Stay in the "Now".

Don't think about the past.
Don't think about the future.

Granted, through our minds we possess an amazing and elaborate time machine. I can zoom back to a childhood memory in a blink. I can get on that vortex of time travel known as YouTube and click on songs from when I was 16....TV shows from when I was a kid...clips of comedians whose bits I used to memorize.

But, I've got to discipline myself. I try to limit my viewing/listening to three clips or songs, and then I have to move onto something in the present.

Perhaps you've got something coming up. A vacation. A holiday. A special event. We have that eager anticipation.

The challenge becomes when we fixate on events in our past, or look ahead to something in the future, which produces negative effects within us.

We revisit some events in our past with regret, resentment or anger.

We dread what may happen in the future, peering into our imaginary crystal ball and predicting the worst that might happen.

This is where it's likely becoming clearer to you that some of these practices that I am suggesting are connected. Almost cousins of each other.

The whole idea of staying in the present is evidenced in Practice #2, The Serenity Prayer.

"God, grant me the serenity to accept the things I cannot change…"

Like the past.

The trick for me is to catch myself when I'm experiencing what is often called, the "Monkey Mind". I have to reign in my thoughts and focus on something in the present.

When I was 23 years old, I picked up a book by Dale Carnegie. Considered a classic, *How to Stop Worrying and Start Living* changed my life. I would encourage you, if you tend to worry, to buy that book. Own it, so that you may have it handy whenever you need a bit of wisdom that lies within its pages.

In thinking about staying in the present, even the Lord's Prayer is about "today". We pray "Give us this day our daily bread...". We're not praying for this week's bread. Or this month's bread. Or, the rest of this year's bread. We're praying for today's bread. No more.

OK. Back to that number. 23,848

What could that mean?

Since the day I was born, 23,848 days have passed as of the date I'm writing these words. That's how many days I've lived through.

And there have been some bad ones. Horrible days that I thought would never, ever end.

I know you can relate.

But, for 23, 848 days, I've made it.

I've survived. I'm still standing.

My mission here isn't complete. I challenge you to do this:

Simply Google "how many days since (insert your birth date)?"

Look at that number.

In spite of all the challenges you've had. All the days that you wish had never happened...

Maybe you still dwell on them.

Look at that number and know that you have survived every single one of them.

You've made it this far. And you didn't make it this far, to only make it this far.

That's what I believe.

Embrace the Boom Practice #5 - Take Nothing Personally

In November of 1997, Don Miguel Ruiz published a book entitled, "The Four Agreements". During a recent check on Amazon, that book is still #1 in the category of "Stress Management".

One of the Four Agreements is one I adopted into my own practices because I believe it is the most difficult one to adopt.

That agreement is, "Take nothing personally."
NOTHING.

We all too often assume that we are the victim of a slight or insult. If we truly have been, isn't it more of a reflection of the offender than us?

While I'm not a psychologist, nor did I stay at a Holiday Inn Express last night, I do know of a psychological principle known as "projection". A classic example of projection is when someone accuses you of a trait that they themselves possess.

A few years ago, I noticed that those who called me a "control freak" were they themselves …well, you know.

Consider the possibility of projection when words start to sting.

Take nothing personally. Simple. Not easy.

Of course, if it's a stranger saying something to me? Whatever. They don't really know me.

But, if it's a friend, a loved one or a family member who says or does something that hits us in the heart.....

Well, . . . then it's most difficult to not take it personally.

For example, let's say a friend didn't invite you to a party you heard about. There's probably a good reason for that. But, you took it personally, didn't you?

Bill Jordan

Maybe the party was for a specific group of people.

Maybe just for old classmates, or just for people in their neighborhood, or just for friends over 6 feet tall.

Who knows?

Here's a nutty idea: Why not just ask them about it?

Perhaps ask if you've offended them in some way? Do you need to make amends? Did you get out of line at the LAST party?

Allow them to feel comfortable enough to be honest with you.

What if it turns out that they just didn't want you there? If that's the case, would you have even wanted to be there?

Sounds like a hassle to me.

I always try to avoid hassles. (I should probably add that to my official list of practices)

DON'T ASSUME THAT WHATEVER SOMEONE SAID OR DID WAS AN INSULT TO YOU.

Something else we tend to do is to say something like this: "I know you're gonna think I'm crazy..."

We assign to them what we think they're thinking. They are probably not thinking anything close to that.

If you are a trusted friend or part of my family then I'm going to listen to you and I'll support you in any way I can.

Two outstanding quotes to wrap this practice up.

The first is actually from the book, *The Four Agreements.*

"There is a huge amount of freedom that comes to you when you take nothing personally."

Pander that a moment.

FREEDOM. That's a tremendous feeling.

The second quote is one of my favorites. It is from a guy who lived a looonnnggg time ago. Marcus Aurelius was a Roman emperor and philosopher. He famously said:

"Choose to not be harmed and you won't feel harmed. Don't feel harmed and you haven't been."

The next time you find yourself on the receiving end of a barbed comment about your clothes, your hair, your age, whatever....

And here's where the practice comes in...

Catch yourself and ask: "Is it really important to respond to this? Do I NEED to take this personally or can I CHOOSE to ignore and let it roll off like water on a duck's back?

Pretend you're a duck.

Bill Jordan

Embrace the Boom Practice # 6 - Two Ears. One Mouth.

This one is a huge reminder for me, as I spent almost 40 years in Top 40 and adult contemporary radio as a disc jockey and morning guy, and now as a voiceover talent. Talking was, and is, my business.

But sometimes, I need my bride or friends to say, "Hey! You're off duty. You can stop now."

Two ears. One mouth.

Here are a few helpful quotes:

"A wise man once said.....nothing."

"It is better to bite your tongue than to eat your words."

"A closed mouth gathers no foot."

"You don't need to attend every argument you're invited to." (And this includes social media.)

Endeavor to listen to understand and not merely to respond.

That's a tall order. We always seem to have our response ready to fly at the very first opportunity.

Sometimes, that listening also includes listening for what is NOT being said.

On another note, I hesitated to include this "condition" of conversation, but I have some select friends, when we get together, often times one of us will say, "I need the Cone of Silence".

As Baby Boomers, we remember the old 60s TV show, "Get Smart". Secret agent Maxwell Smart would go into his boss' office and as they were about to discuss some top secret nonsense, Smart would insist, "Chief, we need the Cone of Silence!". A double headed cone would descend from the ceiling, covering each of their heads. And, of course, being the Cone of Silence, and for comedic effect, neither would be able to hear anything of what the other said. (I loved that bit!)

Whenever a friend or I request the Cone of Silence....

It's not like we don't trust each other on a normal basis, but it transmits that what will be discussed will go no further. Not to a spouse. Not to a mutual friend. No one.

Absolute trust. For our ears only.

We can feel totally free to express our situations, thoughts, fears and hopes. We're in a totally judgement free zone.

Honest feedback is always expected and appreciated.

To paraphrase Proverbs 27:17, "As iron sharpens iron, so one person sharpens another."

If you don't have such relationships in your life with at least one friend or family member, I encourage you to develop two or three. Not many. Just a few with whom may share a rock solid trust.

Choose them wisely.

And never, ever violate their trust in you.

So, there you have it.

Two parts listening. One part speaking.

Sounds like a pretty enticing recipe to me.

Bill Jordan

Embrace the Boom Practice # 7 - Prioritize & Execute

While brainstorming about getting my words down revolving around this whole concept of "Embrace the Boom", I had been focusing on the "execution" part, the "action" part, the "doing" part.

I was discussing this with my bride, Marianne, just before writing this section and she set me straight.

A different perspective.

I like different perspectives.
She said, "You know, for me it's
harder to prioritize than to
execute. Once I prioritize, I've got
no problem with the execution.
It's about coming up with what is
most important."

You know. I think she's right.
(Again.)

Priorities. Deciding on what is
most important.

"I don't have time!"

"I wish I had time!"

"We need to make time!"

"We need to find time!"

The next time you say
something like that, rephrase it
into, "It's just not a priority."

"Getting together with you
guys for dinner? Yeah, just not a
priority."

Certainly, that's not always the case, but many times it is.

If there's something we want to do...

Someone we want to see...

We find a way.

If we don't want to?

We find an excuse.

Sometimes, priorities are crystal clear.

Example: You've got three things to prioritize:

(1) You've got a credit card payment due tomorrow.

(2) Your car needs to be inspected by next month.

(3) You have a grease fire on your stove.

I think I can figure that one out. And pretty quickly. Well, I guess that grease fire just might be my top priority.

The setting of our priorities is often not easy. And it's a very personal thing.

But, for me, if I say that my priorities are my faith, family and friends...

And, I see myself, metaphorically speaking, as a four-legged table....
Physical, mental, spiritual and emotional.

Am I taking care of each "leg" so that I don't wind up with a table that's all wobbly?
I "say" these are my priorities.

Am I truly devoting time tending to these elements of my being?

I plead guilty to not staying on top of them. Think about YOUR priorities.

Give them very serious thought.

Are they in sync with your actions?

Actions (or lack thereof) speak louder than words.

Henry David Thoreau wrote: "It is not enough to be busy. The question is, what are we busy about?"

I am of the opinion that today's society needs to stop its glorification of "busy." I see friends and family fill up their schedules to overflowing. Perhaps so much so that they are missing out on time spent on actions that they "say" are their priorities.

Prioritize and execute.

Decide what is important to you and then follow up with action to make it happen.

Time isn't "found" or "made".

We all have the same amount of time overall. 1,440 minutes each day.

Life comes with commitments that require our time.

But regarding our discretionary time, we need to prioritize it.

Please note, that I'm talking to ME. You're just getting the little speech that I'm giving myself.

A couple more quotes to ponder:

"Time is what we want most, but what we use worst."

                    - William Penn

"Time is free, but it's priceless. You can't own it, but you can use it.

You can't keep it, but you can spend it.

Once you have lost it, you can never get it back."

                    - Harvey MacKay

Bill Jordan

Embrace the Boom Practice # 8 - Be Careful About Giving Up What You Want Most for What You Want Now

This idea is attributed to one of the greatest motivational speakers of all time, Zig Ziglar. In a nutshell, it is the essence of self-discipline, is it not?

It gets back to the other practices you've already read about.

It's a matter of making a choice. Will we choose wisely?

We all get to make choices.

In fact, our lives involve making choice after choice after choice...

So, what do we want most?

What do we "say" we want most?

Have you given this serious thought?

How do you want to be remembered?

How do you want to be physically, mentally, spiritually and emotionally?

Many of us say we want to be in better physical shape, but instead of going for that walk, or going to the gym, or working out at home, we lie down on the couch and binge watch Netflix.

"I'll do a pushup tomorrow."

We say we want to lose weight, but then we knock out a whole pizza and wash it down with a liter of diet cola.

We. Made. A. Choice.

We're constantly negotiating with ourselves.

The ancient philosophers, the guys who lived hundreds of years before Christ, were addressing the exact same human tendencies that we exhibit today. Plato said, "The worst of all deceptions, is self-deception."

That quote has been haunting me for a while.

The serious questions I have to ask myself:

How do I want to be to others?

How do I want to be physically, mentally, spiritually and emotionally?

How do I measure up? Not to others' standards, but to what I claim my own to be?

On what am I negotiating with myself?

Sure, we're all going to have those days when we mindlessly devour a sleeve of Thin Mints.

But, if we can "win" our negotiations with ourselves more often than we "lose", then we'll be less apt to have to say, "My goal is to drop ten pounds this year. Only 15 more to go!"

Be most vigilant about giving up what you want most for what you want now.

Sounds simple.

It is not.

PRACTICE.

"Would you have a great empire? Rule over yourself."

- Publius Syrus

Bill Jordan

Embrace the Boom Practice # 9 - Discipline Equals Freedom

I had a great conversation recently with my grandson Mason. It presented me with an opportunity to share with him the topic of the previous practice - Practice #8: "Try not to compromise what you want most for what you want now."

When I had picked him up for a visit, he immediately asked, "Hey, Poppy! Do we have anyplace we need to go right now?"

"No, Mason. We don't."

"Well, have you ever been in there?" he asked, pointing to a nearby burger joint.

"Uh. Yeah."

"They've got GREAT milkshakes!!! You wanna milkshake, Poppy?!?!?"

"Mason, I "want" a milkshake..."

"You're not gonna get one?!?!?"

"See, there's this thing about not giving up what you want most for what you want now."

Anyway....

He got a milkshake.

We both knew he would.

It was a wonderful chance for a "teachable moment" and I hope that one day he'll remember that.

He's part of the reason why I came up with *Embrace the Boom*.

I'm just trying to get better. And as a byproduct of that, if some of what I'm finding works for me also benefits you (or my grandson) then Mission Accomplished!

Practice #9 is a very close cousin of #8.

#9 is: "Discipline Equals Freedom".

The first time I heard that, I thought that it made absolutely no sense. It sounded contradictory to me.

But, then I got it.

Think of it this way: It kind of goes back to my conversation with Mason.

"Look, Mason. I want to be around for you. I want to be a healthy older guy to see who you become. I want to be around to see you as an adult. I want to live as long as I can live, with the best quality of life I can have."

Now, while I don't get the final say in that, I believe that I do have a vote.

So, here's where discipline equals freedom. I can be disciplined with myself regarding my diet. Maybe healthier and smaller portions for breakfast and lunch. Just a few daily tweaks. Cut back on sugar and liquid calories.

I can be disciplined with my physical activity. There is always something I can do physically everyday. Walk. Stretch. I have several sets of dumb bells of different weights. I have a kettle bell. But it takes more than "having" them. I have to "use" them.

I can set aside time for meditation and/or prayer. I have books with daily entries I enjoy every morning that help anchor me in my core values.

I can also discipline myself with regards to my spending.

The point is, if I take good care of these areas of my life through discipline, then I'll be able to reap the rewards of freedom.

The freedom provided by a stronger and healthier body, mind and soul.

The freedom of some dollars saved and invested that just might allow my wife and me to do a little traveling and to tick off a few of the items on our "Bucket List".

I got this idea from a book entitled, "Extreme Ownership", co-written by two former U.S. Navy SEALs, Jocko Willink and Leif Babin. Phenomenal book. I highly recommend it if you're interested in getting better at anything.

The bottom line is that we get to choose. All throughout the day and at any given moment.

Choose to be disciplined.

Maybe start small. I'm not suggesting that you turn your world upside down.

Little changes to your diet perhaps. Maybe a bit more exercise. Mindful spending. Some quiet time for prayer and/or meditation.

Think of these "disciplines" as investing in yourself.

We can choose the temporary pain of discipline or the long term pain of regret.

Let's choose wisely.

Bill Jordan

Embrace the Boom Practice # 10 - Calm is Contagious (and a Superpower)

Have you ever been to a comedy club?

I'm not talking about watching a video of a comedian performing at a comedy club. I mean actually going to and experiencing in person a comedy club.

If you have, then you know that typically the clubs shoehorn you into that room. You find yourself sitting around a little table about the size of a pie plate. You can perhaps manage to put two glasses and a potato chip on it.

You are crammed in there with everyone else to the absolute maximum that the fire department will allow.

Now, why is that?

There is a huge psychological reason.

Because laughter is contagious. In fact, all emotions are contagious.

Joy can be contagious.

Anger most definitely can be contagious. If someone gets up in your face and starts screaming at you, your natural response is to return anger in kind. We get angry right back at them.

There is one emotion that I believe has proven itself over and over to be a superpower. I can reveal it to you with the very first line in my favorite poem of all time, *IF* by Rudyard Kipling.

"If you can keep your head when all about you are losing theirs and blaming it on you..."

The superpower emotion is CALM.

A sense of calmness.

Calm is contagious.

And I struggle with it.

I can be all relaxed in my recliner, just about to doze off, when the doorbell rings.
Our two dogs, Roxy and Sophie, leap into action, ready to defend our castle. Growling, snarling and barking - in spite of the fact

69

that there has never been, so far, a single threat at the front door. Just dogs doing their job.

It's kind of a weird cycle of events and emotions.

Their fuse gets lit, which lights mine, which in turn gets them even MORE intense.

Crazy.

But, I'm working on it.

Sometimes during the day, when things are going pretty smoothly, I'll just repeat to myself, "Calm is contagious." and "Calm is a superpower.".

And I remember to breathe. Nice, slow, deep breaths.

Do you have a problem with remaining calm?

If you stay calm, those around will tend to remain calm as well.

They will see you as a leader. As someone who has it all together.

Whether you do or you don't, that's how they'll see you.

Just accepting the notion that "Calm is contagious" has allowed me to perhaps be a bit more calm in certain circumstances. I'm better at it than I used to be, that's for sure.

As you adopt any of the *Embrace The Boom* practices, you do become more attuned to noticing your own behavior and thoughts. You're able to catch yourself and correct yourself when your thoughts and actions start to drift towards your old way of thinking and doing.

When you find yourself getting ramped up over

something...you're starting to run off the rails a bit... just remember: Calm is contagious.

Just another one of those simple concepts that can be tough to implement.

That's why they're called "practices".

Embrace the Boom Practice # 11- The 80/20 Rule

First, a little history.

In 1896, Italian economist Vilfredo Pareto showed that approximately 80% of the land in Italy was owned by 20% of the population.

Since then, the "Pareto Principle" has been applied to many arenas in life.

In business management, it is taught that 80% of sales comes from 20% of clients.

In fitness, it's said that 80% of the physical gains you make come from 20% of the time you workout.

One study has even found that 80% of crimes are committed by 20% of criminals.

To apply it in your own life, if you were to make a 10-point "To Do" list, and knocked out the two most important items, you'll likely have an 80% positive impact on your day.

If you have a 5-point list, get the most important thing done and you'll have made a major step forward in your day.

As you might imagine, if we do this every day, great things are going to happen for us.

Try it. See what you think.

Tim Ferris is a podcaster and author whom I really admire. His books include *The 4 Hour Work Week*, *The 4 Hour Body*, *Tools Of The Titans* and *Tribe Of Mentors*.

Tim interviews very successful people and learns what makes them tick.

Remember: Success leaves clues.

My wife, Marianne, and I were watching him on a talk show a few Decembers ago and he was asked if he made New Year's resolutions. He replied that he did not.

But, he revealed that he applies the "80/20 Rule" in his life. Not only pertaining to his activities, but to the people in his life.

Which 20% of his circle bring him 80% of his joy, fulfillment and positivity?

Which 20% bring him 80% of the drama, headaches and negativity in his life?

And then he adjusts accordingly.

Of course, we can't always do this in matters of family or in the workplace. But when we can, I believe it's a worthwhile strategy.

This also applies to social media.

If it eases your mind or emotions to unfollow someone, then consider doing that.

Adopt the 80/20 Rule into your life.

Where could you apply it?

Here's another perspective to think about:

Give serious consideration about where YOU are in someone else's 80/20 Rule.

In which 20% do you reside in their lives?

Hmmmmmmm......

Bill Jordan

Embrace the Boom Practice # 12 - If You Can't Measure It, You Can't Manage It.

Fellow Baby Boomer Jerry Seinfeld, who is three months older than I am, is certainly not "over the hill" or running out the clock.

He's got his wildly successful *Comedians In Cars Getting Coffee* series on Netflix. He still performs stand up, touring nationwide, and where venues often have to add a second show because of the demand.

Jerry Seinfeld is truly "Embracing the Boom".

The story goes that a young comedian came to Jerry and asked, "Jerry, I need some help. I want to write better jokes. How can I do that?".

Jerry replied, "In order to write better jokes, you need to write more jokes. Go to the office supply store and buy one of those big calendars where every day is just a big, blank box. On Day #1, you write a joke and you put a big check mark in that box. Day #2 you write another joke and put a check in that box. After five or six days of doing this practice, you'll have a chain. Then simply, DON'T BREAK THE CHAIN."

The Chain Method.

He setup a system. It's a way to measure it.

Do you want to get in better shape?

If you're doing nothing towards that goal at present, then maybe ease into something just three days a week.

You can measure how far and how fast you walk.

You can methodically increase your distance and speed if you so desire.

(And let me interrupt myself at this point and say you should consult your doctor before starting any new exercise program!)

We get stronger through resistance.

We do not get stronger or better by things being smooth sailing all the time.

I love this line I heard from a motivational speaker, "Son, if the mountain were smooth, you couldn't climb it!"

Maybe you don't consider yourself as a reader, but you want to read more. Try tackling a chapter or two a day.

Focus on reading about a hobby or interest of yours. I truly believe the notion that there is no such thing as someone who doesn't like to read. They just haven't found the right books.

Perhaps you want to strengthen your relationships with friends and family.

Here's a crazy idea: Set a goal of sending out a single handwritten note to a loved one just once a week. Just tell them that you're thinking about them.

How often do we see a friend while we're out and about and promise to each other that we'll get together soon. And then, "soon" doesn't happen.

I get it. "Life" gets in the way. But we do get a vote.

Take the initiative and set up a dinner out or a game night at your house, or go to a concert together.

Bottom line, like everything else, you've got to make it happen.

Have you ever thought of keeping a journal? It doesn't have to be a big deal. You don't have to journal everyday. Just jot down your thoughts about what's going on in your life at the moment. What a gift to your kids and grandkids that might prove to be one day.

The key is STARTING.

Here's the #1 thing we focus on when it comes to Practice #12. WEIGHT LOSS.

You've got to know where you're starting, so . . .
Get. On. The. Scale.

"Oh, I don't know, Bill. That's pretty hard."

Really? It's physically difficult to get on a scale?

No. It isn't.

It may be emotionally tough. Very tough.

That scale doesn't lie. And sometimes the truth hurts. Believe me, I know.

I weigh every Monday morning. This allows me to catch "The Drift". That references the little ounces that creep up on us that turn into pounds. That lead to pants that no longer fit and a physical, AND an emotional self that just feels like crap.

Weighing yourself is certainly one way to measure. Making healthier choices in our diet is another way.

Try one or two hard boiled eggs in the morning instead of the doughnuts.

Dial back on the number of calories in what you drink.

Personally, I haven't had a soda in years, with the perhaps once a year treat of some root beer. Once I stopped drinking it, the desire for it went away; and whenever I have just tasted it since, it isn't appealing at all.

I went on Amazon and typed in "diet." Immediately 90,000 results popped up. I typed in "weight loss" and got back 70,000 results.

When I went to Google in less than a second there were 1,500,000,000 hits for "diet".

Look again at that number just in case you blew by it too quickly.

That's ONE BILLION FIVE HUNDRED MILLION.

Let me remind you of a key bit of wisdom: If nothing changes, nothing changes.

If you can't measure it, you can't manage it.

Decide what you want to accomplish.

Figure out a way to measure your progress.

Remember that the measurement may be adding something and/or subtracting something.

You will begin to celebrate the changes in your life.

Promise.

Bill Jordan

Embrace the Boom Practice # 13 - Keep it Simple

We've all heard of the "K.I.S.S." Method, right?

"Keep it Simple, Stupid".

I'm opposed to that version. I like "Keep it Simple, Smarty."

I believe that words matter and have great power, especially when talking to ourselves. I try not to call myself, "Stupid".

There are plenty of others who will.

Keep. It. Simple.

Leonardo Da Vinci said, "Simplicity is the ultimate sophistication."

If you Google quotes about "simple" or "simplicity" you'll find that there are a ton of them.

Henry Wadsworth Longfellow offered, "Simplicity in character, in manners, in style, in all things. The supreme excellence is simplicity."

Martial artist and movie star Bruce Lee said, "It's not the daily increase, but the daily decrease. We must hack away at the unessential."

What does that mean to you?

Well, it can mean anything you want it to mean. It's all about your choices.

It may mean decluttering your home, your garage, your car, your closet.

It may mean applying Practice #11, the "80/20 Rule". Which 20% of your activities give you 80% of your results?

So, when you look in your closet, ask yourself:

Which 20% of my clothes do I wear 80% of the time?

You may have seen the meme on social media that goes, "I have 150 ball caps and I wear 5 of them." Why do I keep the others?

Perhaps simplify how you spend your time. There are apps that track how much time you spend on your phone and social media.

Are you incessantly checking emails, texts, Twitter and Facebook?

Do you suffer from FOMO? (Fear of Missing Out)

Maybe schedule just a few times a day to check your online social media and email.

Here's one more quote I love. I really want you to contemplate it. It's from Michelangelo.

He was asked about how he came up with his magnificent sculptures.

He answered, "The sculpture is already complete within the marble block. It's already there. I just have to chisel away at the unnecessary." He eliminated everything that didn't look like what he wanted in his final piece.

What do you want to look like?
What do I want to look like?
Not just physically. But, also mentally, emotionally and spiritually.
How do I want to be in these four realms of my existence?
Form a very vivid image in your mind's eye of who and what you want to be.
Then, hack away at the unessential.
Keep it simple.

Bill Jordan

Embrace the Boom Practice # 14 - Today is a Perfect Day for Me to Mind My Own Business

Let's start this practice with a quote from the Roman emperor, Marcus Aurelius:

"To have a good life, we have the potential for it, if we learn to be indifferent to that which makes no difference."

I've looked online and there are several interpretations of

that principle. To me, it just simply means that today is a perfect day to mind my own business.

Mind. My. Own. Business.

How many times have you heard yourself or others say something like:

"Who told her THAT would be an appropriate thing to wear to this event?"

"How can she afford a Mercedes?"

(While in the grocery store) "Ugh! Look what they eat!!!"

We judge all the time.

Here's what I've grown to learn:

When it comes to my intentions and actions, I'm a really good attorney.

When it comes to others' intentions and actions, I'm a really good judge.

That is our nature.

I think it would behoove us to just mind our own.

As long as somebody's not all up in our face or violating any of our rights, I believe that it's the best course of action.

Give it some thought.

The next time something or someone bothers you, and you want to comment and judge, ask yourself, does it really make a difference? Does it really matter to me? Does it affect my life directly?

If it doesn't, then be indifferent to that which makes no difference.

Besides, I've got enough on my plate with out adding to it.

Don't you?

Today is a perfect day to mind my own   business.

Tomorrow will be as well.

Embrace the Boom Practice # 15 - Expect the Unexpected

You and I have lived long enough to know that with a text, a phone call, a scream or a surprise meeting with the boss, life can turn 180 degrees on us.

It can be a nightmare.

And we default, I think, to the negative.

When we talk about "expect the unexpected", it more than

likely references that something bad may happen.

But, reflect a bit on your life. Amazingly good things happen unexpectedly as well.

Maybe you've felt "stuck" in a dead-end job and out of the blue you get an amazing job offer.

Good can spring from bad.

Bad can spring from good.

Always be looking for ways to be the calm in someone else's storm. (Or as my bride reminds me from time to time, just don't be the storm in someone else's calm)

I did the math again a little while ago, and I have been on the planet for 24,000+ days.

I've survived every single one of them. Despite the unexpected, bad and good.

As a follow-up to "expect the unexpected" is "and when possible, BE the unexpected".

In a nutshell, whenever possible, try to leave people, places and things better than when you found them. Here is a simple example:

You pull into the grocery store parking lot and there in the middle of the parking spot you wanted is an abandoned shopping cart. Now, I could moan and groan about it. And believe me, I have.

Or, I can roll that shopping cart right back to the cart corral. Maybe even just use that cart.

It's just a way of taking a negative and turning it into a positive.

Perhaps in that same grocery store you got assistance in finding exactly what you were looking for. (I always need help. Whenever my bride makes out a shopping list, without fail, there is one item that I cannot find)

If you have an especially engaging and funny cashier, how much time out of your day would it take to mosey over to the customer service desk and relay, "Tina over on aisle 7 was exceptional!".

And then leave.

The cashier doesn't need to know you did that. Just do your good deed and be on your way.

Sometimes, surprise your partner or friends with tickets to a special event, or a book you know they'd appreciate. How about a handwritten note just to let them know you're thinking of them.

Just be that little bit of unexpected "positive".

We can leave a situation better than when we found it.

If I'm walking through the kitchen and notice dirty dishes in the sink, I can just stop and wash them.

Sure, I'm a typical husband. "Hey Baby! I just did the dishes! You didn't even have to ask! I washed them all by myself!"

A "Husband of The Year" worthy event, no doubt.

Just strive to leave people, places and things better through your actions.

Well . . . there you go.

My "15 Practices" to lead a better, calmer and more fulfilling life.

That's a wrap.

Or is it?

Embrace the Boom Practice # 16 - Earn This

OK. Wait a second.

I said there were 15 Practices. Here you are, looking at # 16.

"Be the unexpected."

See what I'm doing here?

How do I tie all of these practices together?

Why is there a #16?

Well, the reason is very powerful to me.

Practice # 16 will take all of the previous 15 Practices and add more weight to them.

Practice # 16 is the REAL reason behind trying to live my life by the 15.

To explain it, I need to reference the 1998 movie classic about some members of our Nation's Greatest Generation, "Saving Private Ryan".

In it, you may remember that actor Tom Hanks, as Captain John Miller, leads a squad of U.S. Army Rangers on a mission to find one Private James Ryan, played by Matt Damon.

Ryan's brothers have all been killed during the D-Day invasion. He doesn't know it.

The task is to find Ryan so that he may be sent home, ensuring that his family suffers no further loss.

Along the way, members of the squad are killed in action. They pay the ultimate sacrifice in their quest to save one soldier.

In the next to last scene in the movie, while the Rangers are fighting off a numerically superior Nazi force, Captain Miller is shot and mortally wounded.

He's propped up, and he's dying.

Private Ryan is right there with him.

We see Captain Miller mouth something to Ryan, but we can't hear the words.

Ryan leans in. "Sir?"

Then, Miller reaches out with a shaking hand and grabs Ryan by his uniform.

Pulling him closer, he says, "Earn this. Earn it."

Then, Captain John Miller dies.

The scene ends on Ryan's face.

In a feat of amazing special effects, Ryan is transported to 1998, where as a much older man he is standing in the American cemetery above Omaha Beach in Normandy. He is looking down on Capt. John Miller's gravesite.

He speaks to his rescuer saying, "Every day of my life I've thought about what you said to me that day on the bridge."

Ryan's wife approaches. She doesn't understand what's going on or who this Capt. Miller was.

Ryan turns to her and pleads, "Please tell me I've lived a good life. Tell me I've been a good man."

"You have," she replies. But, she just doesn't understand what happened so many years before that has been burned into her husband's mind and soul.

One powerfully poignant scene.

My Dad was a decorated combat veteran of World War II.

He didn't talk much about it, but when he did, it had a profound effect upon me.

It is not lost on me what he endured and overcame.

Not just in war, but living through the Great Depression.
His hard work to provide for his family.
My Mom worked on the home front, supporting the war efforts. She then dedicated her life to God and her family.

For many of us, we have lived successful and fulfilling lives because of our parents who paved the way.

I hope that I live my life in a manner worthy of their efforts and sacrifices.

I hope that you do.

I hope we all do.

I believe we owe it to them to try to live our very best lives. To be the very best versions of ourselves.

And as we do, I hope that you will...
Live Your Life.
Forget Your Age.
Embrace the Boom.
and ... Earn This.

Acknowledgements

The crafting of this book was certainly not a solo effort.

I'd like to thank my wife Marianne, my daughter Jessica, and my brother Brad for their unfailing support from the very beginning.

Whether it was to get their take on an idea, or helping choose the right word or phrase, they have always been there for me.

Thanks also to Mike Krzyzewski for his most kind words about this effort, and for the 90 minutes he spent with me a few years ago to hear some of my ideas that would evolve into "Embrace the Boom".

A huge thank you to my longtime friend, Mark Grady. Mark patiently walked me through the process of getting a book published, with many laughs along the way.

And a huge thanks to my many Baby Boomer friends and family members who have mentored, encouraged and inspired me along this path.

Live Your Life.
Forget Your Age.
Embrace The Boom.

To follow Bill's continuing journey and to learn how you can receive your very own Embrace the Boom coffee mug, visit:

www.BillJordanEmbracetheBoom.com

To learn more about Bill's voiceover services and listen to commercial and narration demos visit:

www.BillJordanVO.com

CPSIA information can be obtained
at www.ICGtesting.com
Printed in the USA
LVHW031938090322
712946LV00004B/238

9 780981 687247